16.93

D1376355

Mongooses

by Megan Borgert-Spaniol

BELLWETHER MEDIA • MINNEAPOLIS, MN

Note to Librarians, Teachers, and Parents:

Blastoff! Readers are carefully developed by literacy experts and combine standards-based content with developmentally appropriate text.

Level 1 provides the most support through repetition of high-frequency words, light text, predictable sentence patterns, and strong visual support.

Level 2 offers early readers a bit more challenge through varied simple sentences, increased text load, and less repetition of high-frequency words.

Level 3 advances early-fluent readers toward fluency through increased text and concept load, less reliance on visuals, longer sentences, and more literary language.

Level 4 builds reading stamina by providing more text per page, increased use of punctuation, greater variation in sentence patterns, and increasingly challenging vocabulary.

Level 5 encourages children to move from "learning to read" to "reading to learn" by providing even more text, varied writing styles, and less familiar topics.

Whichever book is right for your reader, Blastoff! Readers are the perfect books to build confidence and encourage a love of reading that will last a lifetime!

This edition first published in 2014 by Bellwether Media, Inc.

No part of this publication may be reproduced in whole or in part without written permission of the publisher. For information regarding permission, write to Bellwether Media, Inc., Attention: Permissions Department, 5357 Penn Avenue South, Minneapolis, MN 55419.

Library of Congress Cataloging-in-Publication Data

Borgert-Spaniol, Megan, 1989-
Mongooses / by Megan Borgert-Spaniol.
  p. cm. – (Blastoff! readers. Animal safari)
 Summary: "Developed by literacy experts for students in kindergarten through grade three, this book introduces mongooses to young readers through leveled text and related photos"– Provided by publisher.
Audience: K to grade 3.
Includes bibliographical references and index.
ISBN 978-1-60014-912-2 (hardcover : alk. paper)
1. Mongooses–Juvenile literature. I. Title. II. Series: Blastoff! readers. 1, Animal safari.
QL737.C235B67 2014
599.74'2–dc23

2013000883

Printed in the United States of America, North Mankato, MN.

Contents

What Are Mongooses?

Mongooses are small **mammals**. They have long bodies and short legs.

Mongooses live in forests, **savannahs**, and dry grasslands.

They make homes
in **burrows**.
They also live
in logs and
termite mounds.

termite mound

9

Packs

Some mongooses live in **packs**. They travel together to stay safe.

Adults protect the **pups**. They watch for hawks, jackals, and other **predators**.

Eating

Most mongooses
forage alone.
They use sharp
claws to dig
for **insects**.

They also feed on birds, mice, and other small animals.

Sometimes mongooses eat bird eggs. They throw the eggs at rocks to crack them.

Mongooses even eat snakes. They dodge the snake's bite. Then they attack!

Glossary

burrows—holes or tunnels that some animals dig in the ground

claws—sharp, curved nails at the end of an animal's fingers and toes

forage—to go out in search of food

insects—small animals with six legs and hard outer bodies; insect bodies are divided into three parts.

mammals—warm-blooded animals that have backbones and feed their young milk

packs—groups of mongooses

predators—animals that hunt other animals for food

pups—baby mongooses

savannahs—grasslands with scattered trees

termite—an insect that feeds on wood

To Learn More

AT THE LIBRARY

Halfmann, Janet. *Mongoose*. Detroit, Mich.: Kidhaven Press, 2005.

Pinkney, Jerry, and Rudyard Kipling. *Rikki-Tikki-Tavi*. New York, N.Y.: Morrow Junior Books, 1997.

Sebastian, Emily. *Mongooses*. New York, N.Y.: PowerKids Press, 2012.

ON THE WEB

Learning more about mongooses is as easy as 1, 2, 3.

1. Go to www.factsurfer.com.

2. Enter "mongooses" into the search box.

3. Click the "Surf" button and you will see a list of related Web sites.

With factsurfer.com, finding more information is just a click away.

Index